# Workshop Guide

**Created by**

Dr. Diane Hamilton and Dr. Maja Zelihic

Authors and Creator of

*The Power of Perception*

and

The Perception Power Index Assessment

---

DIMA Innovations
5410 N. Scottsdale Road #C100; Paradise Valley, AZ 85253
DimaInnovations.com and PerceptionPowerIndex.com

# What to Expect in This Workshop

This workshop is designed to give you a framework to understand the importance of perception and how it impacts individual performance. As organizations strive to become more innovative, they must recognize the factors that impact their success. Some of the most critical issues HR professionals, leaders, consultants, and individuals face are tied to the impact of perception. Creativity, engagement, motivation, innovation, and productivity can be improved if we begin by looking at how perception ties to these critical issues.

In this workshop, we will go over the background to what led to the work in The Power of Perception: The Key to Unlocking Human Potential. We will analyze the Perception Power Index instrument as well as the results obtained from taking that assessment. In this workshop, there will be multiple opportunities to create an individual action plan as well as provide input to the organization for what they can do to create a more perception-drive, innovative culture.

Through a series of discoveries published in *The Power of Perception,* we will look at the causes of diminished perception traced to four major characteristics: *Evaluation, Prediction, Interpretation, and Correlation (E.P.I.C.)*

This workshop will enable HR professionals, leadership consultants, other professionals, and individuals to analyze their findings to (1) identify actions they can take to improve their perception; and (2) based on their findings, discuss and recommend company practices their organization can take to improve the overall perception and downstream benefits of its workforce or workforce for which he or she consults.

The intended result of the resulting I-Plan created in this workshop is: (1) an increased corporate focus on improving the perception of its workforce; and (2) a resulting increase in employee engagement, creativity, corporate innovation, productivity, and other known benefits of improved perception.

The implementation of this I-Plan will contain four components:

**1 – The book, *The Power of Perception;***

**2 - The PPI Assessment;**

**3 – I-Workshop and Workbook**

**4 – Corporate Follow-Up from Workshop**

# Phases

The workshop will consist of the following phases:

### *Phase I - Pre-Workshop*

- Each participant agrees to read The Power of Perception: The Key to Unlocking Human Potential
- Each participant agrees to take the PPI Assessment Power Instrument, and receive and review their findings

### *Phase II - The I-Workshop*

- This I-Workshop is to prepare you to:
    - (1) Discuss and explore potential actions to improve their perception based on taking the PPI Assessment Instrument (Participants will not be required to share individual results); and,
    - (2) Discuss and identify recommendations regarding any corporate practices that can enhance the company's perception and downstream benefits of increased creativity, productivity, etc.

### *Phase III - Post-Workshop (for HR professionals, Consultants, and Leadership Professionals)*

- Based on the outputs and recommendations of the I-Workshop, the organization will receive feedback from the activities required in this course.
- The Organization agrees to give serious consideration to enacting the recommendations and provide a response to the participants regarding actions to be taken.

# Benefits of the Workshop

As you read in The Power of Perception, it is critical to understand the benefits individuals receive from improving their perception. Some of those benefits include:

- **Critical thinking** – If we consider critical thinking to mean having the ability to objectively analyze and evaluate to form a judgment, it is crucial to have an open mind that questions content. If we rely too much on Prediction, we impede our ability to think critically.

- **Decision making** – Once we can think critically, we are better prepared to make important decisions based on proper analysis and evaluation. Decisions made in a vacuum can lack insight. Just like an example of a hospital bringing in a pit crew to help with efficiency, decisions can be improved by opening our minds to unconventional ideas.

- **Conflict resolution** – Part of the reason we have conflict is due to lack of empathy, which is a big part of emotional intelligence. There are endless studies that have demonstrated the importance of EI. With five generations in the workplace, conflict has become problematic. Through understanding others' perceptions and viewpoints, we can improve conflict. We can gain that understanding through asking questions and feeling safe to ask those questions.

- **Teamwork** – As teams become more diverse, there are so many advantages to be had based on different levels of experience. However, if people feel uncomfortable sharing insights or asking questions, there can be group think, which can block innovative ideas.

- **Emotional Intelligence** – EI can include things like empathy and interpersonal skills. Part of having people become successful is to improve some of the soft skills and behavioral aspects associated with interpersonal relationships. To get along in the workplace, we must be able to communicate well and put ourselves in other people's shoes. To do that requires asking appropriate questions and listening skills.

- **Employee engagement** – Part of what holds people back from being engaged at work is that they do not see how their job is important to the overall goals of the organization. Employees crave feedback. However, they may hesitate to ask for it. Employees might also be misaligned in their job responsibilities based on what they could be better equipped to perform. Through allowing questions and providing feedback, employees can determine where they would be the best fit for the organization.

- **Innovation** – The advancements in AI will impact the need for more innovation. To be truly innovative requires creativity and motivation. Perception is the spark that leads to the ideas that can be turned into the next innovative ideas. By asking "why not" and "what if", employees can go beyond traditional thinking and become truly innovative.

- **Productivity** – Companies currently lose more than $500 billion a year on lost productivity due to lack of engagement and interpersonal conflict issues. As employees become better communications and more engaged, productivity improves. Perception leads to motivation, which leads to innovation, which leads to improved productivity.

- **Other** – Younger generations want to know how what they do impacts the world. They want to make a difference. By allowing employees to feel safe to be curious, we open the path to communication that can lead to changing the world.

# Factors that Most Impact Perception

Throughout this course, we will refer to EPIC, which is an acronym for the four factors that impact our level of perception. EPIC stands for Evaluation, Prediction, Interpretation, and Correlation.

- *Evaluation* – Evaluation requires that individuals select and organization information from a stimulus. Once attention has been drawn to that stimulus, it is critical to recognize its impact. When individuals interact with others, the signals and information they send cause others to evaluate and organize what they have received. This recognition of how others perceive our intent is a big part of self-awareness, empathy and other factors associated with emotional intelligence. How we respond to cues and analysis of those cues can set us up for success or failure. High levels of emotional intelligence are critical, and yet, CEOs have some of the lowest levels. If leaders are setting the culture of the organization, it is vital that leaders model high levels of EI, and invest in developing levels in their employees. To be good evaluators also requires the ability to think critically. If organizations genuinely desire to have a culture that can thrive in a global climate, developing critical thinking skills and emotional intelligence will be vital.

- *Prediction* - As we make predictions about the meaning of information, we must consider perspectives other than our own. This includes having the ability to interpret how things could be understood by others. There are different vantage points to all situations. How much we care about how we come across to other people can be critical. We often make our predictions based on what we tell ourselves in our minds based on our past experiences. How we make decisions can be problematic if we have incorrect information or have limited experience. That is why being open to alternative viewpoints should be a big part of making predictions.

- *Interpretation* - The third factor the PPI requires we interpret meaning. We process things based on our personal experiences, emotions, reactions to stress and how we read body language or physical traits, as well as many other factors, including religious and political beliefs. Our cultural norms can dictate how we view other people's ways of doing things. Our experience can shape what we see as bad and can cause us to shut down or limit exposure to ideas that are not based on our belief system. We do not have to agree with other viewpoints if we see them as valid base don other people's experiences and cultural norms.

- ***Correlation*** - The fourth and final factor assessed by the PPI is how we make our conclusion based on the correlations we determine are relevant. We must remain emotionally balanced to have strong interpersonal relationships, and to do that, we must consider logic and openness to experience to have a meaningful interpretation. This can be impacted by our sense of happiness, ability to cope, sense of equality and our curiosity. We must include questions as part of how we get to understand one another. By asking questions, we develop empathy When we experience curiosity, we receive a boost of dopamine that can help us feel good. When we have a positive mood and feel emotionally balanced, we can make clear decisions and conclusions. Our conclusions will impact our memory and recall of that situation when it comes to our awareness again. This helps us understand what is needed for potential negotiations.

# Appendix 3: I-Workshop Prediction

This workshop contains the following segments:

- Overview
- 2 Brainstorming Sessions, and
- (An Assessment for HR professionals, consultants, and leadership professionals)
- Conclusions and Follow-Up activities

## About the Creators of this Program

The authors of The Power of Perception and the creator of the Perception Power Index (PPI) are Dr. Diane Hamilton and Dr. Maja Zelihic

## Biography of Dr. Diane Hamilton

Dr. Diane Hamilton is the Founder and CEO of Tonerra, and Co-Founder of DIMA Innovations, which are consulting and media-based businesses. She is a nationally syndicated radio host, keynote speaker, and the former MBA Program Chair at the Forbes School of Business. She has authored multiple books which are required in universities around the world, including Cracking the Curiosity Code: The Key to Unlocking Human Potential, and The Power of Perception: Eliminating Boundaries to Create Successful Global Leaders. She is the creator of the Curiosity Code Index® assessment, which is the first and only assessment that determines the factors that inhibit curiosity and the Perception Power Index, which determines the factors that impact the perception process. Her groundbreaking work helps organizations improve innovation, engagement, and productivity. Thinkers50 Radar chose her as one of the top minds in management and leadership. Her work has been endorsed by some of the most respected names in leadership.

## Biography of Dr. Maja Zelihic

Dr. Maja (Maya) Zelihic is a Fulbright Specialist, Full Professor, and a Department Chair of the Advanced Management Studies at the Forbes School of Business and Interpretation. Dr. Zelihic is a Global Dialogue Partner at NAFSA, the world's largest nonprofit association dedicated to international education. Dr. Zelihic serves on the Board of Advisors of the International Fellowship Program in Arbitration and Scientific Assessment, the comprehensive global academic review platform. She also serves as an industry advisory member at the Amity University Novel Communication Lab (AUNCL). She is an expert in e-learning development and implementation in the developing world. Dr. Zelihic is a Board member at the Center for Women's Leadership at the Forbes School of Business and Interpretation, launched in June of 2020. She is published in over 20+ peer-reviewed journals, and her research ventures took her to Haiti, Cuba, Mexico, Panama, Jordan, Zambia, the Balkan region, and many other parts of the world. In addition to being a Fulbright specialist, she is a four-time recipient of the University Fellows research grants, which enabled many of her global research ventures. Her book on Perception, co-authored with Dr. Diane Hamilton, is scheduled to be released end of this year. Her chapter contribution to the International Leadership Research Handbook is in the final stages of publishing.

# PPI I-Workshop

The workshop contains the following segments:

- Overview
- Two Brainstorming Sessions
- Assessment (for HR professionals, consultants, and leadership professionals)
- Conclusions and next steps

Each of you had a chance to read all or at least part of the book, The Power of Perception, and each of you has taken the PPI assessment and have received your results. Having read the book, you see that each of those aspirations listed are at their core, rooted in perception. And if we can remove the obstacles that impede our perception, those attributes can begin to emerge much more freely.

Further, as you read, those impediments largely center around the four items of:

- *Evaluation*
- *Prediction*
- *Interpretation, and*
- *Our Correlation.*

So, in simple terms, the focus of this brainstorming session is to:

1- *Explore your experiences as it relates to those four items,*
2- *Discuss your observations of your leaders and co-workers and company practices regarding those four items; and,*
3- *Determine what initiatives can be taken to remove those and any other impediments to our perception to improve, within this company, those qualities of:*
    - *Engagement,*

- *Emotional intelligence,*
- *Creativity,*
- *Innovation and,*
- *Productivity*

*As well as the many other attributes that we know stem from perception!*

(Complete introductions).

From reading the book, you know perception is a subject that has been thoroughly examined by behaviorists and educators, as well as business executives, entrepreneurs, and the consulting community. You also probably read that there is a universal consensus among all of them of how perception is at the core of each of the attributes we have spoken about.

What is *new* in our findings, and contained in the latter sections of the book, is what we have learned to be the factors that tend to stop or slow down our perception.

So, our mission here, for those of you who are willing to accept it, is to examine those issues as they affect you personally and your co-workers and leaders and company practices; and get creative about what we can do to remove them.

Our mission, fundamentally, is to improve your company's competitive position in the marketplace through increased perception, and thus innovation and productivity, etc.!

Questions? Comments? Observations?

OK, to get started, our brainstorming session will take place in two exercises:

1 – Using your PPI Assessment results, review the findings and potential actions you would recommend, as it relates to the issues of Evaluation, Prediction, Interpretation, and your Correlation.

2 – A discussion about the general Correlation of your organization (i.e., policies, procedures, practices, norms, etc.), and how the current Correlation encourages or discourages perception, the impact those practices may have on the following activities, and potential actions to improve:

- Critical thinking

- Decision making
- Conflict resolution
- Teamwork
- Emotional Intelligence
- Employee engagement
- Innovation
- Productivity
- Or other

**Exercise #1 – Survey of Actions from the PPI Assessment**

Look at your PPI results regarding:

- Evaluation
- Prediction
- Interpretation, and
- Your Correlation

On page x of your workbook, entitled 'Potential actions to Address E.P.I.C.', based on your own results from the assessment, and the examples in your workbook, list three (or more) you could take in each of the four categories. (Allow 15-20 minutes for this individual activity.)

**Exercise #2 – Survey of Company Practices**

Refer participants to Workbook page Y entitled 'Company Practices Impacting Perception'. The purpose of this exercise is to examine company practices (i.e., norms, practices, policies, regulations, etc.) that both encourage and discourage perception, and the implications or unintended consequences, and potential actions that can be taken, as it relates to:

- Critical thinking
- Leadership
- Conflict resolution
- Teamwork
- Decision making
- Employee engagement
- Creativity

- Innovation
- Productivity
- Or Other

(15-20 minutes (or more, if needed) to consider the company's existing practices, their unintended consequences, and potential actions that could be taken to remedy them)

At the conclusion of the individual or small group sessions, we will reconvene the group to discuss. We can poll individuals for input, first on their findings or observations; then on recommended actions.

The result of this exercise is a composite list of:

A) Company practices that *encourage* Perception;
B) Company practices that *discourage* or hamper Perception;
C) The unintended consequences of those practices, as they relate to Critical thinking, teamwork, conflict resolution, etc., and
D) Recommended actions.

## Module 3: Assessment and Video

**Assessment - HR people**

## Module 4: Wrap Up

**Workshop Summary, Feedback, and Follow-Up Actions**

We know that perception is a critical ingredient as it applies to each of these activities (Point to the list on the whiteboard or flip chart), critical thinking, teamwork, conflict resolution, employee engagement, creativity, innovation, productivity, and so many other activities related to effective organizations.

We now also know that there are four major elements that impact our perception and therefore could hamper those activities.

We know that if we can effectively address those four major elements, we can, therefore, improve these critical activities.

You have just concluded a series of exercises that have the potential to improve those activities in your organization.

Our next step is to summarize this information, including the ideas and recommendations you have come up with today. Your (CEO, Leadership Team, Sponsor) will receive a copy of the completed summary.

Any final thoughts or observations of what we did here today…?'

# Exercise One

In this exercise, we will take three issues from each of the areas of Evaluation, Prediction, Interpretation, and Correlation, to explore from the results of the PPI. Take each issue that came up on your report and create a goal for how you plan to overcome it while making it measurable and considering potential outcomes, support systems, threats and ways to overcome those threats. Later, you can go through all the issues you were not able to address here and do the same for each of them. For now, you will take some time and go through your lowest-rated three issues or the three that seem the most important to you.

| Evaluation Issue | Goal | Time Location | Potential Outcomes | Support System | Potential Threats | Overcoming Threats |
|---|---|---|---|---|---|---|
| **Evaluation Example: Communication** – Keeping our composure when communicating with others who have different viewpoints can be challenging. Taking time to reflect on what caused our emotional reaction can be critical for proper communication. | Ask someone at work or at home, one question showing genuine interest in something that others find interesting. Consider how their viewpoint might differ from your own but still be valid. | Place a note on a calendar or set up an alarm for a convenient time that you know you will be around people, to remember to find someone new each week from whom to learn. | By learning more about things others know, we can build a breath of knowledge we had never considered. We can also learn to develop our sense of empathy, which is a big part of EI. | Ask your friend, peers, and/or family to help you remember to ask them questions. By involving people, it helps us learn new habits because they are there to remind and support us. | Sometimes forgetting to do something can get people off track. | If you find that you have forgotten to ask questions, it is not too late to start the habit again. Use sticky notes, calendar reminders, or alarms if that helps. |

## Evaluation Issue 1: (Example: Communication)

- Goal

- Time/Location (Make it Measurable)

- Potential Outcomes

- Support System(s)

- Potential Threats

- How to Overcome Those Threats

## Evaluation Issue 2:

- Goal

- Time/Location (Make it Measurable)

- Potential Outcomes

- Support System(s)

- Potential Threats

- How to Overcome Those Threats

**Evaluation Issue 3:**

- Goal

- Time/Location (Make it Measurable)

- Potential Outcomes

- Support System(s)




- Potential Threats




- How to Overcome Those Threats

| Prediction Issue | Goal | Time Location | Potential Outcomes | Support System | Potential Threats | Overcoming Threats |
|---|---|---|---|---|---|---|
| **Assumption Example: Alternatives** - We often fail to consider alternatives because we rely on status-quo thinking. This can lead us to draw conclusions before we have all the facts. Knowing when to ask for help is critical. | Go to one person this week to ask their insight on the pros and cons of a decision you need to make. How would they handle researching alternatives? Ask them where they obtain their insights and look outside of your normal resources for ideas. | If you normally read the paper in the morning, use that time to add some additional reading. If not, place a note on a calendar or set up an alarm for a convenient time that you know you will have access to researching a new topic. | By learning more about things that you had convinced yourself were not interesting, you might find that what seemed unlikely to interest you, might spark an interest in this topic or a tangent interest never considered. | Ask your friends, peers, and/or family to join you in learning the new subject. By sharing a common interest, it leads to stimulating chats. | Sometimes things will end up being topics you do not like. | If you find that you are not interested in something, do not let that stop you from learning something different. Not everything is going to interest everybody. |

**Prediction Issue 1:**

- Goal

- Time/Location (Make it Measurable)

DIMA Innovations
5410 N. Scottsdale Road #C100; Paradise Valley, AZ 85253
DimaInnovations.com and PerceptionPowerIndex.com

- Potential Outcomes

- Support System(s)

- Potential Threats

- How to Overcome Those Threats

**Prediction Issue 2:**

- Goal

- Time/Location (Make it Measurable)




- Potential Outcomes




- Support System(s)




- Potential Threats




- How to Overcome Those Threats

**Prediction Issue 3:**

- Goal

- Time/Location (Make it Measurable)

- Potential Outcomes

- Support System(s)

- Potential Threats

- How to Overcome Those Threats

| Interpretation Issue | Goal | Time Location | Potential Outcomes | Support System | Potential Threats | Overcoming Threats |
|---|---|---|---|---|---|---|
| **Interpretation Example: Coping—** When we do not win an argument, we might get upset. It is critical to have healthy responses to how others respond to us. We often can get triggered into emotions that are unproductive. | Think of one challenging interaction you had this week that left you feeling upset. Write down what triggered your emotion and develop a plan for how you will react the next time you and someone else do not agree. | The next interaction you have where you must take a side on a specific idea or argument. | By learning the basics of having foresight and being proactive to uncomfortable issues, can help us cope. | Challenge your friends, peers, and/family to join you in discussion about a topic that you might not feel comfortable discussing with a co-worker. Practice how it might go. | Sometimes people have to agree to disagree. | Do not look at differences of opinion as reasons for failure. |

Interpretation Issue 1:

- Goal

- Time/Location (Make it Measurable)

- Potential Outcomes

- Support System(s)

- Potential Threats

- How to Overcome Those Threats

**Interpretation Issue 2:**

- Goal

- Time/Location (Make it Measurable)

- Potential Outcomes

- Support System(s)

- Potential Threats

- How to Overcome Those Threats

**Interpretation Issue 3:**

- Goal

- Time/Location (Make it Measurable)

- Potential Outcomes

- Support System(s)

- Potential Threats

- How to Overcome Those Threats

| Correlation Issue | Goal | Time Location | Potential Outcomes | Support System | Potential Threats | Overcoming Threats |
|---|---|---|---|---|---|---|
| **Correlation Example: Association** – Many of us came from a time when we were not exposed to different opinions or different cultures. We might associate people's ideas as good or bad. | Next time you run into a discussion where you feel the other person had a closed-minded approach, consider how they might see your idea as inferior and why they might feel that way based on their environment or culture. | Take an hour to research that person's background and culture and focus on the things you have in common and might have different regarding your upbringing or culture. | By leaning into our natural instincts, we can learn information that could set us on a path of discovery toward something we had long forgotten interested us as a child. | Challenge your friends, peers, and/or family to get their insight on why the other person might have such an opposing viewpoint. | Sometimes people have unique personalities or values that we see as negative. | By recognizing others might view our opinions and values as inferior to theirs based on their culture, it can challenge us to communicate in less threatening ways. |

Correlation Issue 1:

- Goal

- Time/Location (Make it Measurable)

- Potential Outcomes

- Support System(s)

- Potential Threats

- How to Overcome Those Threats

## Correlation Issue 2:

- Goal

- Time/Location (Make it Measurable)

- Potential Outcomes

- Support System(s)

- Potential Threats

- How to Overcome Those Threats

**Correlation Issue 3:**

- Goal

- Time/Location (Make it Measurable)

- Potential Outcomes

- Support System(s)

- Potential Threats

- How to Overcome Those Threats

# Exercise Two

Company Practices Impacting Perception - The purpose of this exercise is to examine company practices (i.e., norms, practices, policies, regulations, etc.) that both encourage and discourage perception, and the implications or unintended consequences, and potential actions that can be taken, as it relates to:

- Critical thinking
- Decision Making
- Leadership
- Conflict resolution
- Teamwork
- Employee engagement
- Creativity
- Innovation
- Productivity
- Or Other

| Critical Thinking Decision Making | Leadership | Conflict Resolution | Teamwork | Employee Engagement | Creativity Innovation | Productivity |
|---|---|---|---|---|---|---|
| | | | | | | |

## Topic 1: Critical Thinking

Critical thinking requires objective analysis and evaluation of an issue to form a judgment and to make decisions. Research presented in 2016 found that perception has an impact on decision-making. By piquing people's perception, leaders can have the potential to increase desired behaviors, which can be important for people who might otherwise lack motivation.

In what ways have your leaders and your leaders allowed you to do research, explore ideas, and determine courses of action that could benefit the organization as a whole? Come up with two activities that leaders could do to explore your ability to think critically and make better decisions.

**An example for an idea to present to leadership to improve critical thinking and decision making might be: Allow employees to present a topic of their choice at a weekly meeting. Topics could include ways to improve the way the organization performs a task or be a subject matter expert and explain an area that interests them that no one else really knows well. There is no better way to learn something than to teach it. Explain that employees should try picking a topic that interests them but requires some research and allows them to form a decision about the best way to proceed with some idea based on that research.**

It is your turn to come up with ideas for developing critical thinking and decision making. Be sure to give enough detail so that leaders have a clear idea of the benefit and how to implement the goal by making it measurable. In the prior example, the benefit was to develop critical thinking through exploration of a topic and form a decision based on that research. It is measurable because it states it will occur at a weekly meeting.

- Idea 1:

- Idea 2:

## Topic 2: Leadership

Continue to come up with two ideas for each of the areas listed. In this example, you will come up with two measurable and beneficial ways that leaders can develop their staff to become better leaders through exploring their natural sense of perception.

- Idea 1:

- Idea 2:

## Topic 3: Conflict Resolution

Continue to come up with two ideas for each of the areas listed.  In this example, you will come up with two measurable and beneficial ways that leaders can develop their staff to become better at conflict resolution through exploring their natural sense of perception.

- Idea 1:



- Idea 2:



## Topic 4:  Teamwork

Continue to come up with two ideas for each of the areas listed.  In this example, you will come up with two measurable and beneficial ways that leaders can develop their staff to become better at developing teams by exploring their natural sense of perception.

- Idea 1:



- Idea 2:

## Topic 5: Employee Engagement

Continue to come up with two ideas for each of the areas listed. In this example, you will come up with two measurable and beneficial ways that leaders can develop their staff to become more engaged through exploring their natural sense of perception.

- Idea 1:


- Idea 2:




## Topic 6: Creativity/Innovation

Continue to come up with two ideas for each of the areas listed. In this example, you will come up with two measurable and beneficial ways that leaders can develop their staff to become more creative and innovative through exploring their natural sense of perception.

- Idea 1:


- Idea 2:

## Topic 7: Productivity

Continue to come up with two ideas for each of the areas listed. In this example, you will come up with two measurable and beneficial ways that leaders can develop their staff to become more productive through exploring their natural sense of perception.

- Idea 1:

- Idea 2:

# Lessons and Final Certification Exam

To become certified to give the PPI, you must pass the following test with at least an 80% score. Please read the content under each topic and then answer the question based on what you have learned. Circle the correct answer to the questions listed.

**Question:** Certification entitles you to 6 hours of SHRM recertification credit.

    a. True
    b. False

**Question:** Individuals do not receive an email copy of their PPI results.

    a. True
    b. False

**Question:** There are four major factors that impact perception. These include:

    a. Evaluation, Presumption, Interaction, Conclusion
    b. Empathy, Prediction, Interpretation, Correlation
    c. Evaluation, Prediction, Interaction, Conclusion
    d. Evaluation, Prediction, Interpretation, Correlation

**Question:** There are four major factors that impact perception. Within those factors are _____ subfactors.

    a. 4
    b. 6
    c. 8
    d. 12

---

DIMA Innovations
5410 N. Scottsdale Road #C100; Paradise Valley, AZ 85253
DimaInnovations.com and PerceptionPowerIndex.com

**Question:** There are two major activities required of participants that are important as part of delivering the PPI training.

    a. True
    b. False

**Question:** What is the main site to get information about the PPI?

    a. Perception.com
    b. Ppi.com
    c. Perceptionpowerindex.com

**Question:** Some of the biggest benefits associated with improving perception include the impact it has on:

    a. Critical Thinking
    b. Decision Making
    c. Conflict Resolution
    d. Employee Engagement
    e. Creativity
    f. Innovation
    g. Productivity
    h. Teamwork
    i. Emotional Intelligence
    j. All of the above

**Question:** In the book The Power of Perception, we learned the hormone that makes us bond with people and feel part of something bigger than ourselves is:

    a. Glutamate
    b. Norepinephrine

c. Serotonin
   d. Epinephrine
   e. None of the above

**Question:** In the book, The Power of Perception, we learned what we believe, and what we see and hear has no impact on how we feel, and how we engage others:

   a. True
   b. False

**Question:** This workshop was designed to enable HR professionals, leadership consultants, other professionals, and individuals to analyze their findings to (1) identify actions they can take to improve their perception; and (2) based on their findings, discuss and recommend company practices their organization can take to improve the overall perception and downstream benefits of its workforce or workforce for which he or she consults.

   a. True
   b. False

www.ingramcontent.com/pod-product-compliance
Lightning Source LLC
Chambersburg PA
CBHW080438220526
45465CB00009B/3332